D0999963

DISCARD

Phillis Wheatley

THE INSPRING LIFE STORY OF THE AMERICAN POET

BY ROBIN S. DOAK

COMPASS POINT BOOKS
a capstone imprint

Compass Point Books are published by Capstone,
1710 Roe Crest Drive, North Mankato, Minnesota 56003
www.mycapstone.com

Copyright © 2017 by Compass Point Books, a Capstone imprint.
All rights reserved. No part of this publication may be reproduced in whole
or in part, or stored in a retrieval system, or transmitted in any form or by
any means, electronic, mechanical, photocopying, recording, or otherwise,
without written permission of the publisher.

Editorial Credits
Catherine Neitge and Angela Kaelberer, editors; Ashlee Suker, designer;
Wanda Winch, media researcher; Kathy McColley, production specialist

Photo Credits
Art Resource, NY: Giraudon, 83, Schomburg Center/NYPL, 4, 89;
Bridgeman Images: © Boston Athenaeum, USA/David Claypoole Johnston,
97, © Gavin Graham Gallery, London, UK/Private Collection/William
James, 48; Capstone, 61; The Connecticut Historical Society Museum,
Hartford, Connecticut, 92; Getty Images: Bettmann, 8, 19, 42, 58, Corbis/
VCG/Kevin Fleming, 78, Hulton Archive, 28, 53, MPI, 11, 66, Stock
Montage, 25, 47, UIG/Education Images, 105; Granger, NYC – All rights
reserved, 7, 13, 23, 39, 57, 85, 87, 94, Sarin Images, 34, 37, 71, 81; Library
of Congress: The George Washington Papers, 1741-1799, 75, Prints and
Photographs Division, 14, 51, 91, 98, Rare Book and Special Collections
Division, 62, 101, 102; North Wind Picture Archives, 20, 26, 32, 41, 69, 73,
103, 104; Shutterstock: mcherevan, design pattern; U.S. Senate Collection, 64

Library of Congress Cataloging-in-Publication Data
Names: Doak, Robin S. (Robin Santos), 1963- author.
Title: Phillis Wheatley : the inspiring life story of the American poet / By
Robin S. Doak.
Description: North Mankato, Minnesota : Compass Point Books, an imprint
of Capstone Press, 2017. | Series: CPB grades 4-8. Inspiring stories |
Includes bibliographical references and index.
Identifiers: LCCN 2016004340
ISBN 9780756551667 (library binding)
ISBN 9780756551889 (ebook (pdf))
Subjects: LCSH: Wheatley, Phillis, 1753-1784—Juvenile literature. |
African American women poets—Biography—Juvenile literature. | Poets,
American—Colonial period, ca. 1600-1775—Biography—Juvenile literature.
| Slaves—United States—Biography—Juvenile literature.
Classification: LCC PS866.W5 Z8454 2016 | DDC 811/.1 [B]—dc23
LC record available at https://lccn.loc.gov/2016004340

Printed and bound in Canada.
009644F16

Table of Contents

RO452497639

The enslaved Phillis Wheatley would achieve fame as a poet.

Chapter One

FROM SLAVE TO POET

It was June 17, 1773. The large sailboat *London Packet* moved slowly into the harbor of London, England. After the ship docked, a slender young African-American woman stepped ashore. Nineteen-year-old Phillis Wheatley had last been on a ship 12 years before. But that trip had been very different. Then the little girl had been a captive on a slave ship sailing from Africa to Boston, Massachusetts. That trip had been a nightmare of starvation, disease, and cruelty. But she had survived it. And now she had traveled across the ocean again. This time she was a writer about to have a book of her poems published.

That Phillis Wheatley was about to become a published author was nothing short of amazing. Even the fact that she could read and write was remarkable, for Wheatley was still a slave. At that time in the colonial United States, very few enslaved people were educated. In some colonies teaching a slave to read and write was against the law. Many people believed education would make slaves rebellious and more likely to disobey and run away. But even though John and Susanna Wheatley were slave owners, they treated Phillis well and educated her in their home. When they noticed her talent for writing, they encouraged her and helped get her poems published in newspapers in their hometown of Boston. But no American publisher would consider printing a book of her poems. For that reason the Wheatleys sent Phillis to London. Slavery was still legal in Great Britain as well, but many people there were abolitionists who were working to outlaw slavery. The Wheatleys knew that Phillis would have a much better chance of finding a publisher in Britain.

George III was king of England from 1760 to 1820.

In London people greeted Phillis warmly and treated her as a celebrity. She was invited to parties and other gatherings where she was asked to read her poetry. She received gifts of books and money. She even was invited to meet King George III. It was a life that no one could have expected for her when she had arrived from Africa just a few years earlier.

An auctioneer sold an enslaved African to the highest bidder at a slave auction.

Chapter Two

OUT OF AFRICA

*N*othing is known of Phillis Wheatley's life before July 11, 1761. That day the ship *Phillis* sailed into Boston Harbor in Massachusetts. Instead of cloth, machinery, or tea, the ship's cargo consisted of African-American slaves, mostly from Senegal, Sierra Leone, and islands off the Guinea coast. Many of the slaves who had been kidnapped from their African homes had died during the long, difficult journey across the ocean. But some were still alive, including a little girl about 7 or 8 years old who was missing her front teeth.

The girl was thin, hungry, and sick. She wore only a dirty piece of old carpet as she stood onshore with the other Africans. A slave trader named John Avery looked her over. It was his job to auction off each African for the highest possible price, but he didn't know if anyone would want to buy this small, sickly girl. Still, she was there, and he would try to sell her. Avery advertised the sale in the *Boston Evening Post* and the *Boston Gazette and Country Journal.* The newspaper ad read: "A Parcel of likely Negroes, imported from Africa, cheap for cash, or short credit; … Also, if any Persons have any Negro Men, strong and hearty, tho' not of the best moral character, which are proper Subjects for Transportation, may have an Exchange for small Negroes."

"Small Negroes" meant children, who were the least likely to sell because they couldn't work as hard as adults. Avery was willing to trade children for adult slaves with criminal records who weren't wanted by slave owners in the United States. He could then resell the adult slaves in the Caribbean.

Phillis Wheatley

THE

Boston-

AND

COUNTRY

ntaining the freſheſt Advices,

No. 769.

Gazette,

JOURNAL.

Foreign and Domeſtic.

MONDAY, January 1, 1770.

LIST of the Names of *thoſe* who AUDACIOUSLY continue to counteract the UNIT-ED SENTIMENTS of the BODY of Merchants thro'out NORTH-AMERICA; by importing Britiſh Goods contrary to the Agreement.

John Bernard,
(In King-Street, almoſt oppoſite Vernon's Head.

James McMaſters,
(On Treat's Wharf.

Patrick McMaſters,
(Oppoſite the Sign of the Lamb.

John Mein,
(Oppoſite the White-Horſe, and in King-Street.

Ame & Elizabeth Cummings,
oppoſite the Old Brick Meeting Houſe, all of Boſton.

nd, *Henry Barnes,*
(Trader in the Town of Marlboro'.

HAVE, and do ſtill continue to import Goods from London, contrary to the Agreement of the Mer-nts.—They have been requeſted to Store their Goods on the ſame Terms as the reſt of the Importers have e,but abſolutely refuſe,by conducting in thisManner. T muſt evidently appear that they have prefered their n little private Advantage to the Welfare of Ameri-: It is therefore highly proper that the Public ſhould ow who they are, that have at this critical Time,for-ly detached themſelves from the public Intereſt ; and they will be deemed Enemies to their Country, by all o are well-wiſhers to it ; ſo thoſe who afford them their untenance or give them their Cuſtom, muſt expect to confidered in the ſame diſagreeable Light.

On WEDNESDAY Next the 3d Inſt.
At TEN o'Clock in the Morning,
Will be Sold by PUBLIC VENDUE, at the Store of the late Mr. JOHN SPOONER, next Door Eaſtward of the Heart and Crown.

All his Warehouſe Goods,

Conſiſting of a large Quantity of

KNIVES and Forks, Cuttoes, Shoe Knives, Butchers Knives, all kinds of Penknives, all kinds of Sheara and Sciſſars, Borax, Fountain Pens, Pins, Needles, Ra-zors, Temple and Bow Spectacles, Hand Saws, all ſorts Carpenters Irons and Chizzels, Braſs Ladles, Skimmers, Braſs Candleſticks, Steel Spring Tobacco Boxes, Han-dles and Eſcutcheons, Flatirons, FryingPans, RubStones, Pewter Tankards, Quart and Pint Pots, Poiringers and Tea Pots; all kind of Locks, HL and other Hinges,Com-paſſes, Squares and Rules, Bell-metal and Braſs Skillets, Braſs Kettles made and un-made, 8hoe and Carpenters Hammers, Fire Arms, Piſtols, Stone Sleeve Buttons ſet in Silver, large and ſmall Fiſh Hooks, Gimblets, Tobacco-Tongs, Pincers, Awl & Awl Blades, Braſs head & other Andirons, Steel and Braſs Thimbles, Knitting Needles, Horn and Ivory Combs, Matthewman's Buttons, Beams, Scales and Weights, &c. &c. *A four Wheel Carriage.*
The Sale to continue from Day to Day 'till the whole is Sold. J. RUSSELL, Auctioneer.

BOSTON, 28th of December, 1769.

RUN-away from the Snow Union, John Copithorn, Maſter, from Briſtol, James Clifford and Nicholas Giles, two Seamen.——This is to deſire they will return to their Duty, and they ſhall be well received.—If they do not, to forewarn all Perſons from entertaining them, as they may expect being proſecuted according to Law.

CHARLESTOWN, (South-Carolina,) Nov. 27.
Mr. Gondacre of the 9th regiment, was not kill In a duel with a gentleman from Penſacola, as fo merly mentioned, but with Mr. G—— of ſame regiment, who remains there to take his tri The deceaſed declared himſelf the aggreſſor, and th his antagoniſt was not in the leaſt blameable.
Nov. 9. At a meeting of the general committ on Tueſday laſt, and an adjournment thereof Yeſterday ſeveral matters of importance reſpecti the general agreement entered into by the inhabita of this province on the 22d day of July laſt, we taken into conſideration ; and a committee of inſp tion appointed, whoſe particular buſineſs it will to ſee ſuch Goods imported or re-ſhipped, (at the Opt of the importers) as may be brought here contrary the true intent and meaning of the ſaid agreeme It was at the ſame time agreed, that the general co mittee do meet on Tueſday in every week.
We have the pleaſure to inform our readers, t Mr. Thomas Eveleigh, who arrived here laſt Satur has readily agreed, that the goods which he impor in theFlora, Captain Carter, from Briſtol, ſhall be ſhipped or ſtored : and that Mr. Andrew Marr, done the ſame, in regard to a conſignment of go by the Brigantine Matty, arrived from Glaſgo The ſubſcribers to the reſolutions are ſo conſciou of the juſtneſs of their proceedings, that they gro fuſed to purchaſe ſome ſlaves lately arrived from Pe facola, but alſo rejected a parcel of rice, belonging a gentleman on John's iſland, who is a non-ſubſcrib The few intereſted individuals in the colonies Rhode-iſland and Georgia, who have hitherto miſ thoſe unhappy colonies by ſkim'd milk reaſonin which has been attempted even in our province, hear, have begun to loſe ſo much of their influen

Slave auctions were advertiſed in Boſton newspapers.

Phillis Wheatley never spoke about her capture or her horrible trip across the ocean. But another slave, Olaudah Equiano, told what it was like to be kidnapped. He wrote about how he was captured in Nigeria when he was 11 years old.

II

"[Kidnappers] sometimes took those opportunities of our parents' absence, to attack and carry off as many as they could seize," he wrote. "They stopped our mouths and ran off with us to the nearest wood. Here they tied our hands, and continued to carry us as far as they could, till night came on, when we reached a small house, where the robbers halted for refreshment, and spent the night … being quite overpowered by fatigue and grief, our only relief was some sleep, which allayed [lessened] our misfortune for a short time."

The captors took the Africans to large stone buildings called slave forts. There they held the Africans in tiny, dark rooms with no beds. Some were kept outside in pens like animals. They were given little food or water. When the next slaving ship arrived, their captors herded the Africans down to the shore and rowed them out to the ship.

The living conditions onboard the *Phillis* and other slave ships were horrible. Filth, stench, and disease filled every part of the ship, especially in the hold

Olaudah Equiano was a freed slave who worked to stop the British slave trade.

Captured Africans were packed onto the decks of slave ships.

below the deck. Hundreds of Africans were packed
into that small space. In order to squeeze more in, the
crew chained them side-by-side on wooden bunks. The
head of one African touched the toes of another.

Occasionally the crew took the Africans up on deck for brief periods of fresh air and exercise. Some Africans were so miserable and sick by that point that they chose to commit suicide by jumping over the ship's railing into the ocean.

Phillis probably stayed in a separate hold for children and women, who were often physically abused by the ship's crew. Once or twice a day, she ate a small amount of a thin type of porridge called gruel. Occasionally she might have been given small bits of fish, rice, yams, or beans to supplement the meager gruel.

Disease was the biggest threat to the Africans besides starvation. Diseases such as dysentery, smallpox, and measles spread quickly. The hold areas reeked from the vomit, blood, and other body fluids that covered every inch of space. One out of every four Africans died during the journey across the ocean. On one voyage, a ship carried 167 Africans. When it arrived in North America, only 58 were still alive.

Boston was the capital city of Massachusetts and an important shipping port. It was also home to a thriving trade and manufacturing industry. Of its more than 15,000 people, nearly 1,000 were black slaves. There were also a few black people who had either earned or been given their freedom.

The slave auction of the Africans from the *Phillis* was probably held in late July 1761 at Avery's house in Boston. Many people were likely there that day, most in search of strong adults to work as servants in their homes. Among them were wealthy merchant John Wheatley and his wife, Susanna. John Wheatley owned a warehouse, a wharf, and a large sailboat called the *London Packet*.

Something about the skinny little African girl with the large, sad eyes appealed to Susanna Wheatley. The Wheatleys had two children, 18-year-old twins Mary and Nathaniel. Three of their other children had died at a young age. The youngest, 7-year-old Sarah, had died nine years earlier. The little African girl was about the age of Sarah when she died, and she may have reminded Susanna of her lost child. John Wheatley bought the little girl for what he described as a "trifle." She was too young, small, and sick to bring a high price. The Wheatleys took her to their large home on the corner of King Street and Mackerel Lane in a fashionable part of Boston. King Street was Boston's busiest street, home to many houses and shops. Just a few blocks from the Wheatley house was the Old Colony House, where government officials met to make laws for the Massachusetts Bay Colony.

SLAVE TRADE

Slave traders had been capturing people in Africa long before Phillis Wheatley came to Massachusetts. As early as the 1600s, the west coast of Africa was a center for slave trade. African tribes captured members of enemy tribes and sold them to European and American slave traders. By the 1700s as many as 3,500 Africans were captured and sold as slaves each year. The slave trade provided a lot of money for many Africans, and it became an important part of West Africa's economy. For Americans it meant free labor, especially for the large southern plantations that needed many hands to plant, tend, and harvest crops. Enslaved people worked their entire lives without being paid.

John and Susanna decided to call their new slave Phillis, after the ship that had brought her from Africa. Her last name was Wheatley, since slaves took the last names of their owners.

Phillis certainly already had an African name. But she didn't know a word of English, so the Wheatleys wouldn't have understood even if she had told them what it was. She also couldn't tell them her birthdate and what her life had been like in Africa. Even after she learned English, she never spoke of her earlier life, even about her family and friends. Perhaps they also had been taken and sold as slaves.

The life of a slave was never a good one. But Phillis was more fortunate than many enslaved people. The Wheatleys were kind and treated their slaves and servants well. Phillis would be expected to help around the house, but Susanna wanted to give her an education as well. She hoped the little slave girl would be her friend and companion.

Life at a Glance

DATE OF BIRTH: 1753 or 1754

BIRTHPLACE: Probably modern-day Senegal or Gambia, West Africa

FATHER: Unknown

MOTHER: Unknown

EDUCATION: No formal education; taught by owners

SPOUSE: John Peters

DATE OF MARRIAGE: November 26, 1778

CHILDREN: Three (names unknown); two died as infants, one as a toddler

DATE OF DEATH: December 5, 1784

PLACE OF BURIAL: Unknown

Phillis and the Wheatley family attended church services at Boston's Old South Church.

Chapter Three

LIFE IN A STRANGE LAND

Phillis Wheatley settled quickly into her new home. The Wheatleys treated her more as a member of the family than as a servant. Phillis had her own bedroom, which was unusual. Most house slaves slept in unheated attics or cellars. She may even have eaten at the same table as the Wheatleys, although this isn't known for sure. When the Wheatleys brought her to visit their friends' homes, she sat at a separate table.

It wasn't long before the Wheatleys noticed something special about Phillis. She was intelligent, curious, and learned quickly. John Wheatley was amazed by how quickly she learned English. "Without any Assistance from School Education," he wrote, "and by only what she was taught in the Family, she, in sixteen Months Time from her Arrival, attained the English Language, to which she was an utter Stranger before."

Phillis wasn't satisfied to just learn to speak English. One day the Wheatleys found letters and figures written on the walls with a piece of chalk or charcoal. Phillis had written them, imitating what she had seen the Wheatleys doing. Instead of punishing her, the Wheatleys approved of her desire for education. With her parents' permission, the Wheatleys' daughter, Mary, began teaching Phillis to read and write.

Phillis soaked up knowledge like a sponge. Mary began her reading lessons using the Bible. As her reading ability improved, Mary introduced her to both classical and modern poetry. Phillis also studied geography and history. She even learned French, Latin, and Greek. At the time few girls or women studied languages. Many people believed that girls

To the University of Cambridge, wrote in 1767 —

While an intrinsic ardor bids me write
The muse doth promise to assist my pen.
'Twas but e'en now I left my native shore
The sable Land of errors darkest night
There, sacred Nine! for you no place was found.
Parent of mercy, 'twas thy Powerful hand
Brought me in safety from the dark abode.
    To you, bright youths! he points the height of Heav'n
To you, the knowledge of the depths profound.
Above, contemplate the ethereal space
And glorious Systems of revolving worlds.
    Still more, ye Sons of Science! you've receiv'd
The pleasing sound by messengers from heav'n,
The Saviour's blood, for your Redemption flows.
See him, with hands outstretch't out upon the cross!
Divine compassion in his bosom glows.
He hears revilers with oblique regard
What Condescention in the Son of God!
When the whole human race, by Sin had fal'n,
He deign'd to Die, that they might rise again,
To live with him beyond the starry Sky
Life without Death, and Glory without End. —
    Improve your privileges while they stay:
Caress, redeem each moment, which with haste
Bears on its rapid wing Eternal bliss.
Let hateful vice so baneful to the Soul,
Be still avoided with becoming care.
Suppress the sable monster in its growth,
Ye blooming plants of human race divine
An Ethiop tells you; 'tis your greatest foe

'Tis ——— sweetness turns to endless pain
And ——— eternal ruin on the Soul.

Phillis hoped to publish the poem she wrote at age 14.

only needed to learn how to cook, sew, and run a household. And for a slave—male or female—to have such an education was almost unheard of.

Phillis was receiving an education that was better than what most young white people in Boston had at the time. In her early teens, Phillis translated a Latin poem by the ancient Roman poet Ovid into English. Visitors to the Wheatley home were amazed at her intelligence and ability to talk about many subjects. Many of them encouraged her love of reading by lending or giving her books. One was Mather Byles, who served as the minister of the Congregational Church in Boston. Byles was both a pastor and a poet.

Byles' uncle was Cotton Mather, the respected minister of Boston's Old North Church in the late 1600s. When Mather died, Byles inherited his library. He allowed Phillis to look through the library and borrow books that interested her. He probably introduced her to the works of English poet Alexander Pope. Byles often corresponded with the poet. Pope's poems quickly became Phillis' favorites.

Cotton Mather was a minister and writer.

Phillis also received a religious education. The
Wheatleys were members of the Congregationalist
New South Church in Boston and brought
Phillis to church services with them. Like other
African-Americans, she had to sit in the balcony
during services, away from white churchgoers.

The Old South Church was established in 1669.

As she grew older, Phillis began attending another church, the Congregationalist Old South Church. Phyllis was an active church member. She took her faith seriously and told how it gave her life meaning and purpose. She was baptized in Old South Church in August 1771. The church at that time didn't baptize

A DIFFERENT LIFE

People bought African slaves to do hard work on their farms and in their homes. Slaves worked from dawn until late in the night, seven days a week. But Phillis' life was different. Susanna Wheatley sometimes assigned Phillis light chores around the house, but if Phillis wanted to read a book or write a poem, she could put her chores aside.

Phillis probably felt lonely at times, since she really didn't fit in anywhere. She knew that white people didn't fully accept her as a member of the Wheatley family. The Wheatleys also kept Phillis separate from their other slaves. She wasn't allowed to socialize with the cook, the coachman, or the maid. Once Susanna sent the family carriage to pick up Phillis after she had visited another home. When Phillis returned home, Susanna was horrified to see her riding up front with Prince, the coachman, instead of inside the carriage. It was told that Susanna said, "Do but look at the saucy valet, if he hasn't the impudence to sit upon the same seat as my Phillis."

Phillis was weak and fragile when she arrived in Boston, and she continued to get sick regularly. She suffered from asthma, making it difficult for her to breathe. She may have had tuberculosis, a disease that affects the lungs. The Wheatleys made sure she got constant medical attention. Phillis became so ill one year that Susanna sent her away to recover.

Despite her special privileges, Phillis was still a slave. The Wheatleys were in complete control of her life and her future. They were gentle and kind, but kindness wasn't a substitute for freedom. Phillis had little hope to ever be a free woman.

Samson Occom was a minister and hymn writer.

people until they were at least 18, and Phillis would have been about that age in 1771. It's clear from her poetry that Phillis had developed a strong faith in God.

When Phillis was about 12, she began corresponding with other people. She wrote both to the well-known people who visited the Wheatleys and to friends. She wrote one of her first letters to the Reverend Samson Occom in 1765, when he was on a trip to England.

Occom was an American Mohican Indian who converted to Christianity and became a pastor.

Around the same time, Phillis started writing poetry. Her first poem may have been a four-line poem about the death of two young people in the community, Sarah and Oxenbridge Thacher. A Congregational minister, Jeremy Belknap, included the poem in his 1773 diary, with the title "Phillis Wheatley's first effort—A.D. 1765. A.E. 11." The poem read:

"Mrs. Thacher's Son is gone

Unto Salvation

Her Daughter too, so I conclude

They are both gone to be renewed."

Phillis continued to write poems, many about people whom she knew in Boston. Some were elegies, which expressed sorrow about a person who had died. The Wheatleys were impressed with Phillis' talent. Susanna wrote letters and invited well-known people to the Wheatley home to read the girl's poetry. Susanna submitted one of Phillis' poems to the *Newport Mercury*, a newspaper in Newport, Rhode Island.

The newspaper printed Phillis' poem, "On Messrs. Hussey and Coffin," on December 21, 1767. It was the first time one of Phillis' works appeared in print. She dedicated the poem to ship captain Nathaniel Coffin and his passenger Mr. Hussey, whose first name isn't recorded. The two men once visited the Wheatley

A LIFELONG FRIENDSHIP

Because of her position as a privileged slave in the Wheatley household, Phillis was acquainted with many people but had few close friends. One friend she did have was Obour Tanner.

Tanner was an African-American slave girl about three years older than Phillis. She lived in Newport, Rhode Island, with the Tanner family. Wheatley and Tanner may have come over from Africa on the same ship, but that isn't known for sure.

Like Wheatley, Tanner was owned by a kind family who allowed her to be educated. Tanner wrote her first letter to Wheatley in 1771 or 1772. The two women kept in touch through letters and remained friends until Wheatley's death. Wheatley may have even visited Tanner in Rhode Island. About 10 letters that Wheatley wrote to Tanner survive.

household. They told their terrifying tale of narrowly escaping drowning during a furious storm off Cape Cod, Massachusetts. Phillis wrote the story of their ordeal in verse. The poem also showed the strength of Phillis' religious faith. She wrote:

> *"Suppose the groundless Gulph had snatch'd away*
>
> *Hussey and Coffin to the raging Sea;*
>
> *Where wou'd they go? where wou'd be their Abode?*
>
> *With the supreme and independent God,*
>
> *Or made their Beds down in the Shades below."*

At the age of 14, she wrote "On Being Brought From Africa to America," a poem of gratitude for being brought to the colonies where she could understand about God. She wrote of the "mercy" of being enslaved in order to become a Christian. She reminded Christians that black people can also develop a faith in God.

> *"Twas mercy brought me from my Pagan land,*
>
> *Taught my benighted soul to understand*
>
> *That there's a God, that there's a Saviour too:*
>
> *Once I redemption neither sought nor knew.*

Captured Africans were chained as they waited to be shipped away and sold into slavery.

> *Some view our sable race with scornful eye,*
>
> *'Their coulour is a diabolic die,'*
>
> *Remember, Christians, Negroes, black as Cain,*
>
> *May be refin'd, and join th' angelic train."*

Phillis' poems were about many subjects and people.

She usually didn't write about slavery, but part of her

poem, "To the Right Honourable William, Earl of Dartmouth," described how she felt:

"Should you, my lord, while you peruse my song,

Wonder from whence my love of Freedom sprung,

Whence flow these wishes for the common good,

By feeling hearts alone best understood,

I, young in life, by seeming cruel fate

Was snatch'd from Afric's fancy'd happy seat:

What pangs excruciating must molest,

What sorrows labour in my parent's breast?

Steel'd was that soul and by no misery mov'd

That from a father seiz'd his babe belov'd:

Such, such my case. And can I then but pray

Others may never feel tyrannic sway?"

Phillis may never have talked about her home in Africa or her family, but it's clear from her poem that she remembered the terrible day when she was taken away from them. Her deep sorrow about her past sparked within her a desire for freedom. She longed for her personal freedom, but she also hoped that all other enslaved people would one day be free.

Angry colonists burned paper items bearing British stamps in protest of the Stamp Act.

Chapter Four

GROWING

FAME

Phillis Wheatley and other African-Americans weren't the only people in the American colonies who were longing for freedom. The desire for freedom from British rule was growing every day.

The British Parliament passed the Stamp Act in 1765. It required colonists to buy a stamp for almost everything written or printed on paper. Newspapers, wills, deeds, and even playing cards had to be stamped. The colonists were furious. They felt the British government had no right to impose the tax. After all, the colonists had no one representing them or speaking for them in Parliament. Angry

mobs formed in the streets of Boston. They stole from
the homes of British officials and threatened anyone
who supported the new tax. Some protesters beat up
tax collectors or chased them out of Massachusetts.
Some people even started talking about becoming
independent from Britain. They became known
as patriots.

Other colonists supported more peaceful ways
of protest. They decided to talk directly to British
lawmakers. Benjamin Franklin was one such person.
He helped form the Stamp Act Congress, which
encouraged colonists not to pay the stamp tax. Finally,
the British Parliament repealed the Stamp Act. For a
while the colonists were satisfied.

But by 1768 Britain had passed more tax laws,
angering the colonists again. Massachusetts was the
center of the protests, and its colonial governor,
Francis Bernard, asked the British government for
help. Britain responded by sending 4,000 soldiers to
Boston to enforce the laws and keep order. Bostonians
were angry that the red-uniformed British troops were

British soldiers occupied the city of Boston.

in their city. Colonists called the soldiers names such as "redcoats" and "bloodybacks."

Fights continued to break out in the city. A crowd of people gathered February 22 at the house of Ebenezer Richardson, a colonist who was loyal to Britain.

Earlier that day Richardson had tried to stop a protest at the shop of loyalist merchant Theophilis Lillie. The protesters chased Richardson back to his house and began throwing rocks at the windows, breaking them. One of the rocks struck Richardson's wife. Richardson fired on the crowd, striking and killing 11-year-old Christopher Seider, also spelled Snider. Colonists were outraged over the death of someone so young. About 5,000 people attended the funeral that patriot Samuel Adams organized for Seider.

But the worst clash happened the evening of March 5, 1770. About 300 to 400 colonists were yelling insults and throwing rocks, sticks, and snowballs at several British soldiers outside the Custom House on King Street, just down the street from the Wheatley home. The soldiers opened fire on the crowd, killing three colonists and wounding eight. Two of the wounded later died. The first colonist killed was Crispus Attucks, who was of African-American and American Indian heritage. Colonists called the incident the Boston Massacre.

Colonists and soldiers fought outside the Custom House in the Boston Massacre.

Seventeen-year-old Phillis wrote poems about both events. She first penned "On the Death of Mr. Snider Murder'd by Richardson," in which she called young Christopher the "first martyr for the cause." After the Boston Massacre, she wrote "On the Affray in King Street, on the Evening of the 5th of March, 1770," which was printed in the *Boston Evening Post*. Although her name wasn't published with the poem, people who knew her recognized it as her work. The poem honored four of the fallen colonists, including Attucks.

"Long as in Freedom's Cause the wise contend,

Dear to your unity shall Fame extend;

While to the World, the letter's Stone shall tell,

How Caldwell, Attucks, Gray, and Mav'rick fell."

From these poems and others like them, it seems that Wheatley was a supporter of the American independence movement. She may have hoped that if the colonists became free of British rule, they would consider freeing their slaves as well.

Not all of Wheatley's poems were about current events or politics. Many were written about or dedicated to people who had died. Such poems were called elegies, and they were popular at the time. People believed they gave comfort to the family and friends of the deceased person. An elegy Wheatley wrote early in October 1770 gained her a great deal of attention. The 62-line poem "An Elegiac Poem, on the Death of that Celebrated Divine, and Eminent Servant of Jesus Christ, the Late Reverend, and Pious

George Whitefield

George Whitefield," was written about the famous British minister George Whitefield. He often traveled to the colonies, preaching to crowds of thousands of people. He was a gifted speaker with a booming voice that people claimed could be heard from a mile away. Whitefield had preached in Boston in August 1770, and Wheatley most likely went to hear him. His message agreed with Wheatley's strong religious beliefs.

Whitefield died unexpectedly September 30 in Newburyport, Massachusetts, a town about 35 miles (56 kilometers) northeast of Boston. Wheatley must have immediately picked up her pen—her completed elegy was advertised in the *Boston News-Letter* newspaper October 11. A portion of it praises the great preacher:

"Hail, happy Saint, on thy immortal throne!

Whitefield was a popular preacher in England and the colonies.

To thee complaints of grievance are unknown;

We hear no more the music of thy tongue,

Thy wonted auditories cease to throng.

Thy lessons in unequal'd accents flow'd!

While emulation in each bosom glow'd;

Thou didst, in strains of eloquence refin'd,

Inflame the soul, and captivate the mind."

The elegy was signed "By Phillis, a servant girl
of 17 years of age, belonging to Mr. J. Wheatley, of

Boston:—And has been but 9 years in this country from Africa."

John and Susanna Wheatley had the poem printed as a broadside, a large sheet of paper printed on one or two sides. The broadside was sold as a pamphlet throughout Boston for the price of "seven coppers." Later the poem was printed in newspapers in New York City, Newport, Rhode Island, and Philadelphia, Pennsylvania. It was printed in London in 1771.

Phillis' talent amazed people. Many stopped by the Wheatley home to meet the unusual slave girl who wrote beautiful poetry. One of them was George Whitefield's friend Thomas Woolbridge, who later wrote, "While in Boston, I heard of a very Extraordinary female Slave, who made some verses on our mutually dear deceased Friend [Whitefield]; I visited her mistress, and found by conversing with the African, that she was no Imposter; I asked her if she could write on any Subject; she said Yes."

Susanna Wheatley decided in 1772 that more people needed to read Phillis' poems. She tried to get them published as a book. In February, March, and April, she ran advertisements in the *Boston Censor* for a book of 28 poems. The advertisement listed the poems Wheatley wrote about Christopher Seider, the Boston Massacre, and the arrival of British troops in Boston. It also included her tribute to George Whitefield and several other elegies.

In colonial times a book was often advertised in newspapers before it was published to see if enough people were interested in buying it. If not enough people responded to the ads, the publisher might choose not to publish the book, saving the cost of printing a book that wouldn't sell. The Wheatleys hoped that at least 300 people would say they were interested in buying the book.

Susanna's ads got few responses. Some people even doubted that Phillis had written the poems. At the time many people believed that black people were less intelligent than whites. They didn't believe a black slave girl could possibly write so well.

The Wheatleys knew that if they ever wanted to get Phillis' poems published in a book, they had to stop the rumors and doubts about her. In the fall of 1772, John Wheatley asked some of the most respectable men in Boston to meet with Phillis and judge whether the poems were her own. Eighteen well-known men, most of them slaveholders, agreed to question Phillis and examine her poetry. The group included ministers, politicians, judges, and authors.

No written records exist of the meeting, so no one knows exactly what the men said to Phillis. But they probably asked her questions about Greek mythology, the Bible,

A CLASSICAL EDUCATION

Wheatley included references to the Bible and Greek mythology in many of her poems. She wrote about several ancient classical poets, including Homer and Virgil, in her 1773 poem "To Maecenas."

The poem also includes a verse about the Roman playwright Terence, who died in 159 BC. Terence was born in Africa, possibly in Libya or Tunisia. He was brought to Rome as a slave, where his owner educated and later freed him. Wheatley could only hope that might happen to her.

and well-known works of literature. They also may have asked her to write a poem on the spot. Whatever the questions were, Wheatley was able to answer them, proving that she was an educated, intelligent young woman who was more than capable of writing poetry. The impressed group of men agreed to sign a statement that said, "We whose Names are under-written, do assure the World, that the Poems specified in the following Page, were (as we verily believe) written by Phillis, a young Negro Girl, who was but a few Years since, brought an uncultivated Barbarian from Africa, and has ever since been, and now is, under the Disadvantage of serving as a Slave in a Family in this Town."

The 18 signatures include those of Massachusetts governor Thomas Hutchinson and lieutenant governor Andrew Oliver. Patriot and merchant John Hancock and poet Joseph Green signed it, as well as Phillis' old friend Mather Byles.

The support of the well-known citizens was important for Phillis. It also may have changed some

John Hancock confirmed that Wheatley wrote her own poems.

colonists' ideas about black people. People who supported freedom and equal rights for blacks pointed to Wheatley and asked why blacks were being enslaved if they could accomplish the same things as whites.

But even with her growing fame and the support of well-known people, no American publisher was willing to take a chance on Phillis' book of poetry. To accomplish that, she had to make another journey across the ocean. This time she would go to England.

Wheatley stayed in London on her trip to England in 1773.

Chapter Five

SUCCESS

IN ENGLAND

Three years before she traveled to England, Phillis Wheatley had made an important friend there. Selena Hastings, Countess of Huntingdon, was an abolitionist and a supporter of George Whitfield. When Wheatley wrote her elegy for Whitfield, she mentioned the countess by name in the final verses:

"Great COUNTESS! we Americans revere

Thy name, and thus condole thy grief sincere:

We mourn with thee, that TOMB obscurely plac'd,

In which thy Chaplain undisturb'd doth rest."

Wheatley also sent the countess a copy of the poem, along with an appreciative letter. The countess liked Wheatley's tribute to her friend, and she agreed to help Wheatley get her poems published in England.

The Wheatleys had another reason for sending Phillis to England. She had been sick much of the previous two years. Doctors had told the Wheatleys that a sea voyage might help her recover. The Wheatleys decided not to go with Phillis to England. Instead their son, Nathaniel, would go with her. He recently had taken over his father's company and had business in London.

Wheatley was excited about her trip and wrote about her feelings in a poem before she left. Although her poem reflected her anticipation of the trip, it also expressed her sadness at leaving the Wheatleys in Boston. She dedicated "A Farewell to America" to Susanna:

> *"Susannah mourns, nor can I bear*
> *To see the crystal show'r,*
> *Or mark the tender falling tear*
> *At sad departure's hour."*

Phillis and Nathaniel left Boston on the Wheatleys' ship, the *London Packet*, on May 8, 1773. The trip took more than a month, and they arrived in London on June 17.

During her six weeks in London, Phillis saw many sights, including two famous museums, the British Museum and Cox's Museum. She toured Westminster Abbey, the church where kings and queens were

The British Museum was established in 1753.

EDITORIAL CHANGES

Because it was published in London, Wheatley's book of poetry ended up being different from what it would have been had it been published in the colonies. The titles of some of the elegies were changed, because the British wouldn't be familiar with their subjects. Patriotic poems such as the ones about Christopher Seider and the Boston Massacre weren't included, because they were critical of the British government. Instead the book included poems favorable toward Britain such as "To the King's Most Excellent Majesty, 1768." Wheatley wrote the poem after King George III repealed the Stamp Act.

crowned, married, and buried, as well as the Royal Observatory at Greenwich, a science center. British abolitionist Granville Sharp took her to the Tower of London, where English kings and queens had lived for centuries. The Tower featured collections of royal crowns and jewels, as well as a zoo of live animals such as lions, tigers, and wolves. Phillis also attended the theater for the first time in her life, enjoying musical and dramatic plays at London's famous theaters.

Wheatley would later remember her trip to England as the best time of

The Thames River flows through London, England.

her life. She wrote to Obour Tanner about how the British treated her:

"The friends I found there among the nobility and gentry. Their benevolent conduct towards me, the unexpected and unmerited civility . . . with which I was treated by all, fills me with astonishment, I can scarcely realize it."

Phillis and Nathaniel also had many visitors at the London apartment where they were staying. One was Benjamin Franklin, who had helped convince Britain to repeal the Stamp Act. Franklin was living in London at the time as a representative of the colonial government. Franklin's nephew Jonathan Williams, who lived in Boston, asked him to visit Phillis while she was in London. But the meeting didn't go to Franklin's liking. He thought that Nathaniel Wheatley didn't want him there. Franklin later wrote to Williams:

"Upon your recommendation I went to see the black Poetess and offer'd her any Services I could do her. Before I left the house I understood her master was there, and had sent her to me, but did not come into the room himself, and I thought was not pleased with the visit. I should perhaps have inquired first for him; but I had heard nothing of him, and I have heard nothing since of her."

It's not clear why Nathaniel Wheatley refused to meet with Franklin. His parents had urged Williams to write to Franklin about Phillis. Perhaps he disagreed with Franklin's political views.

Phillis had a chance to meet another famous person while in London. In mid-July she was invited to the royal palace to meet King George III. He was not a popular person in the colonies. Colonists blamed the king for the taxes and strict rules that they had lived under for several years. But being granted an audience with King George III was still an honor. Before Phillis could meet with the king, though, she received word that Susanna Wheatley was dying. Phillis canceled her visit to the palace and arranged to return home

A CHANCE FOR FREEDOM

Wheatley was still a slave when she arrived in England. But if she had decided to stay there, she would have done so as a free woman. A ruling by a British high court in 1772 outlawed the right of slave owners to seize their slaves and force them to return to their home countries.

Legally, no one, including the Wheatleys, could have forced Phillis to return to the colonies. No one knows if Phillis considered this fact when she heard of Susanna Wheatley's illness. If she did, her loyalty to Susanna must have convinced her that she needed to see Susanna before she died.

on the *London Packet* in late July. Nathaniel stayed in London, where he later married a British woman, Mary Enderby.

Wheatley also never got the chance to meet the Countess of Huntingdon, who was sick and had left London for her home in Wales. Wheatley was disappointed not to meet her benefactor. She wrote a letter to the countess July 17, saying, "[I am] extremely reluctant to go without having first seen your Ladyship."

But even though Wheatley was sad to leave England earlier than she planned, she knew Susanna needed her. She boarded the *London Packet* on July 26 for the long trip home. As soon as the ship docked in Boston on September 13, 1773, Phillis hurried to the Wheatley home. At the time Susanna was only expected to live a few days. But she clung to life for several more months. Phillis stayed at Susanna's side and wrote letters on her behalf since Susanna was too weak to pick up a pen.

Susanna Wheatley lived long enough for one of her dreams to come true. In December 1773 copies

Selina Hastings, Countess of Huntingdon

of Phillis' book, *Poems on Various Subjects, Religious and Moral,* arrived in Boston. Susanna had recognized Phillis' intelligence and talent from the beginning. Now the little girl she had nurtured and taught was a published author.

A colorized version of the drawing of Phillis Wheatley that appeared in her book

Chapter Six

SADNESS
AND SUCCESS

No one knows exactly when Phillis Wheatley became a free woman. But in October 1773, she wrote to a friend, David Wooster: "Since my return to America my Master, has at the desire of my friends in England given me my freedom." It's believed that John Wheatley freed her shortly after she returned from England. He signed a deed of manumission, which was an official document giving Wheatley her freedom. She continued to live in the Wheatley household and help care for Susanna.

Susanna Wheatley died March 3, 1774. Phillis grieved deeply for her friend and companion. Susanna may have been Phillis' owner, but she was also her strongest supporter and the closest thing to a mother she had since she was kidnapped from Africa. Phillis wrote to Obour Tanner about her sadness:

"I have lately met with a great trial in the Death of my mistress; let us imagine the loss of a Parent, Sister, or Brother, the tenderness of all these were united in her.—I was a poor little outcast & stranger when she took me in, not only into her house, but I presently became a sharer in her most tender affections. I was treated by her more like a child than her servant."

In another letter to Tanner, Wheatley wrote that she felt "like one forsaken by her parent in a desolate wilderness. I fear lest every step should lead me into error and confusion."

Wheatley had dedicated *Poems on Various Subjects, Religious and Moral* to the Countess of Huntingdon. It was the first book of poetry published by an

Wheatley was born in Africa but lived most of her life in Boston.

African-American. In fact, Wheatley was one of the first African-Americans to publish any kind of book.

Her British publisher, Archibald Bell, knew that many people would doubt that a slave could write a book of poetry. He included the statement signed by the men who had questioned Wheatley in Boston.

FAMOUS PORTRAIT

The Countess of Huntingdon decided Wheatley's picture should appear inside the front of her book. Instead of an oil painting, an artist did an ink sketch of Phillis. The sketch was later made into the engraving that appeared in the book. The artist's name is unknown, although it may have been Boston artist and fellow African slave Scipio Moorhead. Wheatley later wrote a poem about Moorhead's paintings. Like the Wheatleys, Moorhead's owners encouraged his talents. When Scipio's owner, John Moorhead, died in December 1773, Wheatley composed an elegy for him.

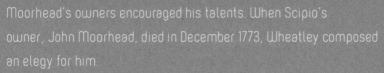

Wheatley's portrait reflects her roles as both a slave and a writer. She wears servant clothes, including an apron and a hat. She holds a quill pen in her right hand, as if she is about to start writing a new poem. She gazes into the distance, with a thoughtful expression. Around the oval frame of the picture are the words, "Phillis Wheatley, Negro Servant to Mr. John Wheatley, of Boston." Today the portrait of Phillis Wheatley hangs in the Smithsonian Institution's National Portrait Gallery in Washington, D. C.

Bell wrote in the book's preface:

"The following poems were written originally for the Amusement of the Author, as they were the Products of her leisure Moments. She had no Intention ever to have published them; nor would they now have made their Appearance, but at the Importunity of many of her best, and most generous Friends; to whom she considers herself as under the greatest Obligations."

People had various opinions about Wheatley and her poetry. Voltaire, the famous French author, historian, and philosopher, praised Wheatley's book, saying that her work proved that blacks could write poetry. But some people weren't impressed with her writing. A London reviewer wrote that the poems "display no astonishing power of genius," but were remarkable because a black slave wrote them. Another person said that her poems had no fire or spirit.

Some people disliked the book because a black person had written it. They claimed she must have imitated another writer. Thomas Jefferson was one

Thomas Jefferson criticized Wheatley's writing.

of these critics. Jefferson, who later helped write the Declaration of Independence and became president of the United States, wrote, "Religion, indeed has produced a Phillis Whatley [sic]; but it could not produce a poet. The compositions published under her name are below the dignity of criticism."

Many people were upset about Jefferson's comments. Several came to Wheatley's defense, including Presbyterian minister Samuel Stanhope Smith. He wrote a response to Jefferson: "The poems of Phillis Wheatley, a poor African slave, taught to read by the indulgent piety of her master are spoken of with infinite contempt. But I will demand of Mr. Jefferson, or of any other man who is acquainted with American planters, how many of those masters have written poems equal to those of Phillis Wheatley?"

Wheatley's book inspired many black colonists. Another educated black slave and poet, Jupiter Hammon, wrote a poem in Wheatley's honor called "An Address to Miss Phillis Wheatley." In the poem, Hammon said Wheatley was a role model for the young people of Boston.

Wheatley's book sold well in England. Copies were sent to the American colonies and European countries. Wheatley quickly became the most famous African-American in Europe and the colonies. Her future seemed bright.

P O E M S

O N

VARIOUS SUBJECTS,

RELIGIOUS AND MORAL.

BY

PHILLIS WHEATLEY,

NEGRO SERVANT to Mr. JOHN WHEATLEY, of BOSTON, in NEW ENGLAND.

LONDON:

Printed for A. BELL, Bookseller, Aldgate; and sold by Messrs. COX and BERRY, King-Street, BOSTON.

M DCC LXXIII.

The title page of Phillis Wheatley's book

chapter Seven

FREEDOM AND A REVOLUTION

For Phillis Wheatley, freedom brought new responsibilities. For the first time, she was in charge of her future. She needed to find a way to make a living as a free black woman in Boston. John Wheatley said she could still live at the Wheatley home, which Phillis appreciated. She wrote to a friend, "I hope ever to retain a grateful sense, and treat him with that respect which is ever due a paternal friendship."

Wheatley did have one way to support herself— she was a published author with a book to sell. She received half the price of each book sold. She worked hard to sell more copies of her book, writing to friends and acquaintances and asking others in person if they would buy her book. Obour Tanner also asked people to buy the book and was able to sell six copies. Samson Occom sold some as well.

But it was a bad time to be peddling books. Colonists had more on their mind than reading. Anger against the British government was reaching a boiling point, especially in Boston.

In late March 1774—just a few weeks after Susanna Wheatley's death—the British Parliament passed a series of laws called the Coercive Acts. The acts were meant to punish Massachusetts patriots. They had protested the British tax on tea by dumping a shipment of British tea in Boston Harbor in December 1773. Parliament hoped that the new laws would coerce the Massachusetts colonists back into obedience. But that didn't happen.

The furious colonists called the new laws the Intolerable Acts. One law closed Boston Harbor on

Boston was a major site of resistance to British authority.

June 1, with no colonial ships allowed to enter or leave. British Army General Thomas Gage became the governor of Massachusetts Colony, with the sole authority to appoint government officials. Town meetings were restricted in the colony to one each year unless the town had special permission from the governor. Gage also had the power to send any

British officials who were charged with crimes in Massachusetts back to Britain for trial. More British soldiers arrived in Boston, forcing colonists to house and feed them if other lodging wasn't available.

Representatives from every colony except Georgia met in September 1774 in Philadelphia, Pennsylvania. The meeting was known as the First Continental Congress. The representatives agreed to stop trading with Britain. They also said colonists no longer had to obey British laws that took away their freedoms as citizens.

The growing tension between the colonists and the British government exploded April 19, 1775. Seven hundred British soldiers arrived at Boston Harbor and marched to Lexington, Massachusetts. They were going to Concord, Massachusetts, to search Colonel James Barrett's farm for weapons. At Lexington, 77 colonial soldiers were waiting for them, and shots were fired. British troops continued to Concord, where more than 300 patriots were ready to fight. On their way back, the patriots attacked the British, and the

The Battle of Lexington sparked the beginning of the Revolutionary War.

battle spread. Soldiers on both sides were killed, but the British retreated and returned to their ships in Boston Harbor. The Revolutionary War had begun.

Many Bostonians felt that their city was no longer safe. In the spring of 1775 Mary Wheatley and her husband, John Lathrop, left Boston for Providence, Rhode Island. John Wheatley joined them several months later. There's no record if Phillis went to

Rhode Island with the Wheatleys, but it's likely that she did.

Members of the Continental Congress met again in May. They decided the colonies needed an army, and chose George Washington of Virginia to lead it. Washington left Philadelphia and headed for Boston. News spread quickly throughout the colonies about Washington and his army of about 14,500 soldiers. They had neither training nor official uniforms.

Wheatley had hoped for a peaceful end to the problems between Britain and the colonies. She had good memories of England and its people, but she supported the colonies. She wanted them to be free of Britain's rule. As always, she put her feelings into poetry. Her patriotic poetry won her the admiration of many colonists.

Wheatley wrote a poem in Washington's honor that she titled "To His Excellency General Washington." She mailed it to him at his headquarters at Cambridge, near Boston, in October. She included a letter that told Washington how glad she was that

George Washington took charge of the Continental Army in 1775.

he was commanding the Continental Army and humbly apologizing for any mistakes that the poem might contain. She ended the letter, "Wishing your Excellency all possible success in the great cause you are so generously engaged in."

Part of her poem read:

"Proceed, great chief, with virtue on thy side,

Thy ev'ry action let the goddess guide.

A crown, a mansion, and a throne that shine,

With gold unfading, WASHINGTON! be thine."

Wheatley received a reply from Washington in February 1776. In the midst of a raging war and a difficult winter, the general took time to answer her letter and praise her poetry. He thanked her for the poem and apologized for not responding sooner:

"[A]s a tribute justly due to you, I would have published the poem, had I not been apprehensive, that, while I only meant to give the world this new instance of your genius, I might have incurred the imputation [accusation] of vanity. … If you should ever come to Cambridge, or near headquarters, I shall be happy to see a person so favored by the Muses."

It's not known whether Phillis ever met Washington. If she was in Providence with the Wheatleys, she might have met him in April 1776, when Washington passed through the city on his way to New York.

A reproduction of Washington's letter to Wheatley

Washington did send Wheatley's poem about him to his former secretary, Colonel Joseph Reed. He suggested to Reed that he submit the poem for publication, because Washington didn't want people to think he was bragging about himself by seeking its publication. Reed sent the poem to the *Virginia Gazette*, which published it in March 1776.

STILL NOT FREE

When Wheatley was in England, people she met there couldn't understand why an intelligent, artistic person like her was still a slave. English critics were quick to write harsh essays about John Wheatley. But they also wondered how Americans could still be enslaving people when they were fighting for their own freedom from Great Britain.

One man wrote: "We are much concerned to find that this ingenious young woman is yet a slave. The people of Boston boast themselves chiefly on their principles of liberty. One such act as the purchase of her freedom would, in our opinion, have done them more honor than hanging a thousand trees with ribbons and emblems."

The writings of such educated British people likely had an influence on John Wheatley. They may have encouraged him to give Phillis her freedom.

The Continental Army surrounded Boston by early March, forcing the British soldiers to leave the city. The Wheatleys and other Boston residents could now return to their homes. But the city had changed a great deal. British soldiers had chopped down most of the trees for firewood. When the trees were gone, the soldiers tore down wooden buildings. One of those buildings was the Old North Church, where John Lathrop was the minister. The Wheatley home also suffered major damage when colonial cannon fire struck it by accident.

The colonists were fighting a war for independence, but they still hadn't formally declared themselves independent of Great Britain. That changed July 4, 1776, when members of the Continental Congress voted to adopt the Declaration of Independence. Phillis and others hoped that this step would bring the country one step closer to freedom. She wrote about her country using the poetic name "Columbia."

"Celestial choir! enthron'd in realms of light,
Columbia's scenes of glorious toils I write.
While freedom's cause her anxious breast alarms,
She flashes dreadful in refulgent [splendid] arms.
See mother earth her offspring's fate bemoan,
And nations gaze at scenes before unknown!"

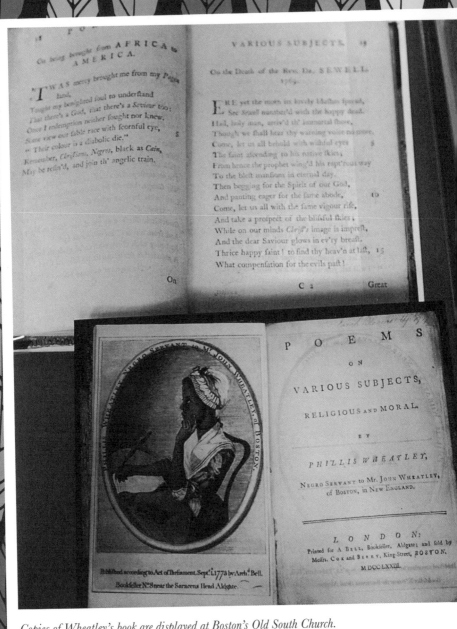

Copies of Wheatley's book are displayed at Boston's Old South Church.

Chapter Eight

LATER
YEARS

The Wheatley family returned to Boston in December 1776. Although it was a happy time for the family, it marked the beginning of difficult times for Phillis. John Wheatley died March 12, 1778. Mary Lathrop, Phillis' teacher and friend, died just a few months later at age 35. For the first time since she had come to the colonies as a slave, Phillis was alone in the world.

John Wheatley didn't leave any money or possessions to his former slave in his will. Phillis wasn't sure where she would live or how she would earn her living. Few jobs were open to women at that time, since most women were expected to marry and spend their lives caring for their houses and families. Life was even more difficult for free black women. Free blacks had to compete with white people for jobs. Sometimes free blacks even competed with black slaves whose masters hired them out to earn more money. Slavery was becoming less accepted in Massachusetts, but white people generally preferred to give jobs to other white people.

Wheatley had many friends throughout the colonies, but with the war raging on, they were busy with their own lives and problems. She also had had friends in England, including Nathaniel Wheatley, but the war made communication with them difficult. All of these reasons may have influenced Phillis to make a big decision. When a free black man named John Peters asked her to marry him, she said yes.

Little is known about Peters' early life or when he and Phillis met. Peters was a free man, but it's not known if he was born into freedom or if he was a freed slave. He ran a grocery store on Court Street in

A deed of manumission granted freedom to enslaved people.

Boston. Some said he also worked as a tailor, a baker, a physician, and even a lawyer, sometimes arguing cases for other blacks in the city. He was described as handsome, intelligent, and well mannered. One person called him "a remarkable specimen of his race, being a fluent writer, a ready speaker." Such qualities may have been what persuaded Phillis to accept his marriage proposal.

Phillis and John were married November 26, 1778, at the Second Congregational Church in Boston. John Lathrop, the widower of Mary Wheatley, performed the ceremony. Phillis moved into Peters' house on Queen Street.

Although Phillis had a place to live, that didn't mean that her life was secure. Soon after the marriage, Peters' store went out of business. He went into partnership with a white man, Josias Byles, to sell grain and other goods in western Massachusetts. While he was gone, Phillis remained in Boston and continued to write poetry. But Peters' partnership with Byles went sour, and Peters filed and won a lawsuit against Byles to recover money and goods that he owed Peters. But Peters himself was then successfully sued by a woman who may have supplied him and Byles with the goods that they sold. Even the judgment that he won from Byles wasn't enough to cover this debt.

With her husband out of work and in debt, Phillis needed to find a way to make money. She continued to try to sell copies of her first book. In 1779 she also

Wheatley's husband had worked at several businesses in downtown Boston.

tried to get a second book of poetry published. She ran six advertisements in local newspapers to see if there were enough people interested in buying the book. The ads described a 300-page volume, dedicated to "Right Hon. Benjamin Franklin, Esq: One of the Ambassadors of the United States at the Court of France." It would be longer than her first book and would feature 33 poems and 13 letters. But when few people responded to her ads, she had to give up the idea.

Phillis lost touch with many people after her marriage. But she did continue to write to her old friend Obour Tanner, even though Tanner didn't approve of Phillis' marriage to Peters, saying "poor Phillis let herself down by marrying." Phillis wrote to Tanner in Worcester, Massachusetts, on May 16, 1779:

"By this opportunity I have the pleasure to inform you that I am well and hope you are so; tho' I have been silent, I have not been unmindful of you, but a variety of hindrances was the cause of my not writing to you. But in time to come I hope our correspondence will revive—and revive in better times—pray write me soon, for I long to hear from you—you may depend on constant replies."

No one knows if Tanner answered the letter or if the two ever saw each other again. The circumstances of Wheatley's life may have prevented her from continuing the friendship.

HER TRUE FEELINGS

Once Phillis Wheatley was no longer a slave, she could write openly about what she thought of slavery. She wrote a letter to her friend Samson Occom in February 1774. In it she compared American slaves to the Israelite slaves in Egypt during biblical times. The letter was published in many area newspapers in 1774. Part of it said: "In every human Breast, God has implanted a Principle, which we call Love of Freedom; it is impatient of Oppression, and pants for Deliverance; and by the Leave of our modern Egyptians I will assert, that the same Principle lives in us."

Wheatley also commented on the hypocrisy of the colonists who were fighting for America's freedom while at the same time enslaving a whole race of people. She described it as "the strange Absurdity of their Conduct whose Words and actions are so diametrically opposite." The letter was one of the first antislavery letters written by a black person in the colonies.

I am very affectionately your Friend
Phillis Wheatley
Boston-March 21. 1774.

Wheatley and her husband may have left Boston in 1780 for the village of Wilmington, Massachusetts, which is about 15 miles (24 km) from Boston. They may have moved both to escape the battles being fought in and around Boston and to avoid John Peters' debt collectors. In May 1778 France agreed to help the Americans fight for independence. Fighting increased with the arrival of the French army, and life in Boston and other large cities became more dangerous. Many people fled the cities for smaller country towns.

No one is sure about Wheatley's life in Wilmington. It's believed that she and John had three children while they were there, and that the first two died as babies. No birth or death records exist for the children, but that wasn't unusual at the time, especially for free black people. More accurate records exist of slaves, whose births, marriages, and deaths were recorded in detail by their owners.

As the Revolutionary War dragged on, things started to improve for the American side. In late September 1781 about 17,000 American and

The British surrender at Yorktown marked the end of major fighting in the war.

French soldiers surrounded British General Charles Cornwallis' 9,000 soldiers at Yorktown, Virginia. After three weeks of steady American cannon fire, Cornwallis surrendered October 19. Minor skirmishes continued to occur, but Yorktown was the last major battle of the war. The British government realized that the Americans weren't going to give up their fight for freedom. The Treaty of Paris officially ended the war September 3, 1783. The 13 American colonies were now the United States of America, a free and independent country.

Wheatley celebrated the event with a poem titled "Liberty and Peace." The poem was published as a pamphlet early in 1784. Part of it reads:

"E'en great Britannia sees with dread Surprize,

And from the dazzling Splendor turns her Eyes!"

By this time Wheatley had moved back to Boston. One account said she came back without her husband and lived for six weeks with Susanna Wheatley's niece Elizabeth Wallcut. John Peters may have abandoned his family for a time. Or he may have been serving time in a debtor's prison. In any case, Wheatley had to support herself and her remaining child.

Wheatley took a job as a maid at a boardinghouse. Even though she had grown up as a slave, she wasn't used to hard physical labor. She still had the health issues that had caused her problems her entire life. The work that she was now trying to do weakened her even more. With her new responsibilities, Wheatley had little time to write poetry. Only four of her poems

Wheatley's hard work as a maid was bad for her health.

were published during the last eight years of her life, all of them in 1784.

John Peters eventually returned to Boston, and the family moved into a run-down apartment. Phillis was still responsible for supporting her family. She tried one more time to publish a second book of poetry, placing an ad in the September 1784 issue of *Boston Magazine.* It included a previously unpublished poem titled "The Poem [To Mr. and Mrs.—On the Death of Their Infant Son."] But like her earlier proposal, the advertisement didn't create enough interest for a publisher to take on the expenses of printing her poems in a book.

But there were people who were still interested in Wheatley's work. One of them was the famous British minister John Wesley, who helped found the Methodist religious denomination. In July 1784 he published Wheatley's poem "An Elegy on Leaving—" in the *Arminian Magazine.* The poem is about a person's regret about having to leave a peaceful place in the country. It's not known when Wheatley wrote the poem, but its theme is both sad and hopeful. She may have been expressing her sadness over her current life and the hope that it could still get better with these lines:

"But come, sweet Hope, from thy divine retreat,
Come to my breast and chase my cares away,

John Wesley was a prominent minister.

> *Bring calm Content to gild my gloomy seat,*
> *And cheer my bosom with her heav'nly ray."*

Wesley was one of the few people who seemed to still care about Phillis and her poetry. The wealthy and influential friends she had made when she lived with the Wheatleys had disappeared from her life. Sadly, she realized that no help was coming from them. She shared her feelings in a letter to a friend, John

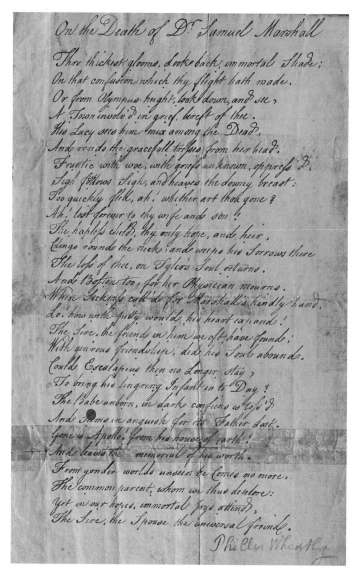

Wheatley wrote many elegies.

Thornton: "The world is a severe Schoolmaster, for its frowns are less dang'rous than its Smiles and flatteries, and it is a difficult task to keep in the path of Wisdom. I attended, and find exactly true your thoughts on the behavior of those who seem'd to respect me while under my mistresses patronage: you said right, for Some of those have already put on a reserve."

Wheatley's health continued to fail. On December 5, 1784, she died at the boardinghouse where she was living. She was 31 years old, broke, and alone, except for her small child. John Peters was likely again in debtors' prison. Very soon after Phillis' death, her child also died. They were probably buried together in Boston, but no one knows exactly where. A death notice in the newspaper *Independent Chronicle and Universal Advertiser* said Phillis' funeral was to be held December 9, at the home of Dr. Thomas Bulfinch in Boston. Bulfinch's house was near the Granary Burial Ground, where the Wheatley family was buried, so Phillis and her child may be buried there. The grave is unmarked, so no one knows for sure. It was a sad ending for a life that once held so much promise.

PHILLIS WHEATLEY

CA 1753-1784

BORN IN WEST AFRICA AND SOLD AS A SLAVE
FROM THE SHIP *PHILLIS* IN COLONIAL BOSTON,
SHE WAS A LITERARY PRODIGY WHOSE 1773 VOLUME
*POEMS ON VARIOUS SUBJECTS, RELIGIOUS,
AND MORAL* WAS THE FIRST BOOK PUBLISHED BY
AN AFRICAN WRITER IN AMERICA.

A bronze statue of Phillis Wheatley is part of a display at the Boston Women's Memorial.

Chapter One

A PLACE
IN HISTORY

*n*ews of Phillis Wheatley's death was printed in several newspapers throughout Massachusetts and the surrounding states. The articles highlighted her accomplishments, such as her poetry. Few mentioned that she was a former slave or that she had died in poverty and was buried in an unknown grave.

After Phillis died, John Peters wanted to make money off her work. He placed a newspaper ad in February 1785 asking the person who had borrowed the unpublished manuscript of Phillis' proposed last book to return it to him so it could be published. Peters apparently never got the manuscript back, and only one of the unpublished poems listed in Phillis' book proposal has ever been found. Peters died in 1801, still in debt.

At least two publishers reprinted Wheatley's only book of poetry after her death. But soon people forgot about Wheatley and her poetry. In the 1830s, however, abolitionists working to end slavery rediscovered her poetry. They used her as an example of what blacks might accomplish if they were given the opportunity. At the time many people still believed that black people weren't as intelligent as whites. Abolitionists held up Wheatley's intelligence and writing talent to disprove that opinion.

Some of Wheatley's poems were published in *Memoir and Poems of Phillis Wheatley* in 1834. Thirty years later *Letters of Phillis Wheatley, the Negro Slave-Poet of Boston* was published. At a time when slavery was dividing the country, Wheatley's poetry gave encouragement to people who were fighting against it. After the Civil War (1861–1865) the 13th Amendment

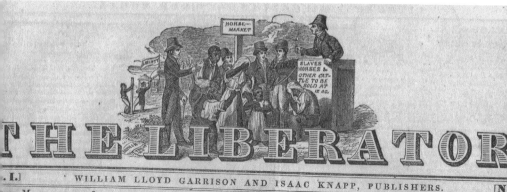

THE LIBERATOR

WILLIAM LLOYD GARRISON AND ISAAC KNAPP, PUBLISHERS.

OUR COUNTRY IS THE WORLD—OUR COUNTRYMEN ARE MANKIND.

Wheatley's poetry appeared in The Liberator, *an abolitionist newspaper.*

to the U.S. Constitution finally outlawed slavery in the entire United States.

African-Americans were no longer enslaved, but they still didn't share equal rights and status with white people. They often weren't allowed to vote, attend school, or to work in well-paying jobs. As

Poet James Weldon Johnson was critical of Wheatley's work.

African-Americans worked to gain their civil rights, opinions about Wheatley began to change.

In the 1920s many people criticized Wheatley for not being angrier about being kidnapped from Africa and shipped to North America to become a slave. They were also upset that she hadn't spoken out more strongly against slavery. African-American poet and author James Weldon Johnson wrote in 1922

AN ELEGY FOR PHILLIS

Throughout her life Phillis Wheatley honored many people who had died with elegies. After her death an elegy was written for her. A poet who used the name Horatio published a 54-line elegy called "Elegy on the Death of a Late Celebrated Poetess" in the December 1784 issue of *Boston Magazine*.

Horatio must have known about Wheatley's difficulties during her later years. He also must have known about her strong faith in an eternal life. The elegy ends:

"Tho' now the business of her life is o'er,
Tho' now she breathes and tunes her lyre no more;
Tho' now the body mixes with the clay;
The soul wings upward to immortal day;
Free'd from a world of wo, and scene of cares,
A lyre of gold she tunes, a crown of glory wears."

about Wheatley's poetry, "one looks in vain for some outburst or even complaint against the bondage of her people, for some agonizing cry about her native land."

Others said that Wheatley's fame wasn't due to her writing talent. They said she only became famous because she was a black woman writing at a time when most blacks in America were enslaved and unable to read or write.

In the 1960s black leaders involved in the civil rights movement spoke out strongly against Wheatley and her poetry. They thought she accepted the way that whites viewed blacks and that her work was a reflection of white, rather than African-American, culture.

In recent years people have taken another look at Wheatley's poetry. Many say her poems shouldn't be judged on whether their viewpoint is black or white. Wheatley's poems provide a unique perspective on the time in which she lived. In an era when most people didn't think slavery was wrong, Wheatley shared feelings from a slave's point of view. At the same time, she had a level of access to white society that was unusual in the 1700s. In many ways she lived in two worlds and could offer valid viewpoints on both.

Phillis Wheatley made her mark on history as the first African-American poet to publish a book. In her short life, she wrote nearly 150 poems about a variety of topics. She is an important symbol of what people can do when they are given the chance to shine.

Phillis Wheatley, America's first black poet

Timeline

1767
First published poem is printed in the *Newport Mercury*, a Rhode Island newspaper

1753 OR 1754
Born in Africa

1765
Writes first known letter to the Reverend Samson Occom

1761
Kidnapped in Africa and taken to Boston, Massachusetts; sold as a slave to John Wheatley

1772

Interviewed by 18 respected Bostonians to determine if she is capable of writing poetry

1770

Writes poem about the Boston Massacre

1773

Travels to England; Poems on *Various Subjects, Religious and Moral* is published; granted her freedom

1771

Baptized at the Old South Church in Boston

Timeline

1776
Receives letter from George Washington and may have visited him

1774
Owner Susanna Wheatley dies

1778
Marries John Peters; owner John Wheatley dies; teacher Mary Wheatley Lathrop dies

1775
Writes a poem in honor of George Washington

1779–82

Has three children, two
of whom die as babies

1782

Moves back to Boston;
works as a maid

1779–80

Efforts to publish a second
book of poetry fail; moves to
Wilmington, Massachusetts

1784

Dies December 5
alone and penniless in
Boston boardinghouse,
followed by her
youngest child

Glossary

abolitionists—people who supported the banning of slavery

apprehensive—fearful; worried

asthma—lung disorder that makes it difficult to breathe

coerce—persuade by force or threats

correspond—to communicate by exchanging letters

denomination—religious group

dysentery—serious infection of the intestines marked by severe diarrhea

elegy—poem expressing sorrow for one who is dead

impudence—quality of being offensively bold

intolerable—so harsh or bad it cannot be accepted

manumission—the act of freeing from slavery

martyr—person who gives his or her life for a cause

massacre—the deliberate killing of a group of helpless people

Parliament—part of the British government that makes laws

patriot—person who sided with the colonies during the Revolutionary War

smallpox—contagious disease that causes the skin to break out in blisters and leave deep scars

trifle—small amount

Further Reading

Aloian, Molly. *Phillis Wheatley: Poet of the Revolutionary Era.*
New York: Crabtree Publishing Company, 2013.

Marciniak, Kristin. *The Revolutionary War: Why They Fought.*
North Mankato, Minn.: Compass Point Books, 2016.

Marcovitz, Hal. *The History of Slavery.*
San Diego: ReferencePoint Press Inc., 2015.

Taylor, Charlotte. *Phillis Wheatley: Colonial African-American Poet.*
New York: Enslow Publishing, 2016.

Internet Sites

Use FactHound to find Internet sites related to this book. All of the sites on FactHound have been researched by our staff.

Here's all you do:

Visit www.facthound.com

Type in this code: 9780756551667

OTHER BOOKS IN THIS SERIES

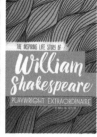

Source Notes

Page 10, line 10: William H. Robinson. *Phillis Wheatley and Her Writings*. New York: Garland, 1984, p. 5.

Page 12, line 1: M.A. Richmond. *Bid the Vassal Soar: Interpretive Essays on the Life and Poetry of Phillis Wheatley (ca. 1753-1784) and George Moses Horton (ca. 1797-1883)*. Washington, D.C.: Howard University Press, 1974, p. 13.

Page 17, line 4: Henry Louis Gates Jr. *The Trials of Phillis Wheatley: America's First Black Poet and Her Encounters With the Founding Fathers*. New York: Basic Civitas Books, 2003, p. 17.

Page 22, line 1: Ibid., p. 19.

Page 27, line 15: *Phillis Wheatley and Her Writings*, p. 24.

Page 29, line 10: Vincent Carretta. *Phillis Wheatley: Biography of a Genius in Bondage*. Athens: The University of Georgia Press, 2011, pp. 46–47.

Page 31, line 6: *Phillis Wheatley and Her Writings*, p. 129.

Page 31, line 18: *The Trials of Phillis Wheatley: America's First Black Poet and Her Encounters With the Founding Fathers*, p. 70.

Page 33, line 3: "To the Right Honourable William, Earl of Dartmouth." Academy of American Poets. 28 April 2016. https://www.poets.org/poetsorg/poem/right-honourable-william-earl-dartmouth

Page 39, line 4: "Phillis Wheatley Writes about Christopher Seider." Boston 1775. 4 May 2007. 28 April 2016. http://boston1775.blogspot.com/2007/05/phillis-wheatley-writes-about.html

Page 40, line 3: "The Case of a Slave Poet, A Forgotten Historical Episode." IIP Digital. U.S. Department of State Bureau of International Information Programs. 26 March 2002. 28 April 2016. http://iipdigital.usembassy.gov/st/english/texttrans/2005/09/20050901140626pssnikwad0.6985895.html#axzz3yNqo9stF

Page 41, line 21: "Phillis Wheatley. An Elegiac Poem, On the Death of that Celebrated Divine, and Eminent Servant of Jesus Christ, the Late Reverend, and Pious George Whitefield." Boston: Russell and Boyles, 1770. A Celebration of Women Writers. Penn Libraries. University of Pennsylvania. 28 April 2016. http://digital.library.upenn.edu/women/wheatley/whitefield/whitefield.html

Page 43, line 6: *Phillis Wheatley: Biography of a Genius in Bondage*, p. 73.

Page 43, line 14: *Phillis Wheatley and Her Writings*, p. 23.

Page 46, line 7: Ibid., p. 28.

Page 49, line 8: Julian D. Mason Jr., ed. *The Poems of Phillis Wheatley*. Chapel Hill: University of North Carolina Press, 1989, p. 134.

Page 50, line 19: Phillis Wheatley. *The Collected Works of Phillis Wheatley*. New York: Oxford University Press, 1988, p. 120.

Page 53, line 3: *The Poems of Phillis Wheatley*, p. 198.

Page 54, line 9: *Phillis Wheatley and Her Writings*, p. 36.

Page 56, line 8: John R. Tyson. *In the Midst of Early Methodism: Lady Huntingdon and Her Correspondence*. Lanham, Md.: Scarecrow Press, 2006, p. 223.

Page 59, line 4: *Phillis Wheatley and Her Writing*s, p. 40.

Page 60, line 7: Ibid., p. 37.

Page 60, line 15: Ibid., p. 45.

Page 63, line 1: *The Collected Works of Phillis Wheatley*, preface.

Page 63, line 15: *The Poems of Phillis Wheatley*, p. 24.

Page 64, line 2: *The Trials of Phillis Wheatley: America's First Black Poet and Her Encounters With the Founding Fathers*, pp. 42 and 44.

Page 65, line 4: *Bid the Vassal Soar: Interpretive Essays on the Life and Poetry of Phillis Wheatley (ca. 1753-1784) and George Moses Horton (ca. 1797-1883)*, p. 53.

Page 67, line 7: *The Poems of Phillis Wheatley*, p. 210.

Page 73, line 3: *The Trials of Phillis Wheatley: America's First Black Poet and Her Encounters With the Founding Fathers*, p. 37.

Page 74, line 1: Ibid., p. 39.

Page 74, line 10: *Phillis Wheatley and Her Writings*, p. 53.

Page 76, line 8: Ibid., p. 39.

Page 77, line 12: "Enclosure: Poem by Phillis Wheatley, 26 October 1775." Founders Online. National Archives. 28 April 2016. http://founders.archives.gov/documents/Washington/03-02-02-0222-0002

Page 81, line 5: Phillis Wheatley: Poetry Foundation. 28 April 2016. http://www.poetryfoundation.org/bio/phillis-wheatley

Page 84, line 7: *Proceedings of the Massachusetts Historical Society*, Vol. 7. 1863-1864. Boston: John Wilson and Son, 1864, p. 268.

Page 84, line 10: Vincent Carretta, ed. *Complete Writings. Phillis Wheatley*. New York: Penguin Books, 2001, p. 162.

Page 85, lines 6 and 12: *The Trials of Phillis Wheatley: America's First Black Poet and Her Encounters With the Founding Fathers*, p. 73.

Page 88, line 6: Phillis Wheatley. "Liberty and Peace." Boston: Warden and Russell, 1784. A Celebration of Women Writers. Penn Libraries. University of Pennsylvania. 28 April 2016. http://digital.library.upenn.edu/women/wheatley/liberty/liberty.html

Page 90, line 20: *Phillis Wheatley: Biography of a Genius in Bondage*, p. 189.

Page 92, line 1: Ibid., p. 145.

Page 99, sidebar, line 10: *Phillis Wheatley and Her Writings*, p. 64.

Page 99, line 1: *The Trials of Phillis Wheatley: America's First Black Poet and Her Encounters With the Founding Fathers*, p. 75.

Select Bibliography

Academy of American Poets. https://www.poets.org

A Celebration of Women Writers. Penn Libraries. University of Pennsylvania.
http://digital.library.upenn.edu/women/writers.html

Bassard, Katherine Clay. *Spiritual Interrogations: Culture, Gender, and Community in Early African American Women's Writing*. Princeton, N.J.: Princeton University Press, 1999.

Boston 1775. http://boston1775.blogspot.com

Carretta, Vincent, ed. *Complete Writings. Phillis Wheatley.*
New York: Penguin Books, 2001.

Carretta, Vincent. *Phillis Wheatley: Biography of a Genius in Bondage.*
Athens: The University of Georgia Press, 2011

"The Case of a Slave Poet, A Forgotten Historical Episode." IIP Digital. U.S.
Department of State Bureau of International Information Programs. 26 March 2002.
28 April 2016. http://iipdigital.usembassy.gov/st/english/texttrans/2005/09/20050
901140626pssnikwad0.6985895.html#axzz3yNqo9stF

Founders Online. http://founders.archives.gov

Gates, Henry Louis, Jr. *The Trials of Phillis Wheatley: America's First Black Poet and Her Encounters With the Founding Fathers*. New York: Basic Civitas Books, 2003.

Mason, Julian D., Jr., ed. *The Poems of Phillis Wheatley.*
Chapel Hill: University of North Carolina Press, 1989.

Poetry Foundation. http://www.poetryfoundation.org

Proceedings of the Massachusetts Historical Society, Vol. 7. 1863–1864.
Boston: John Wilson and Son, 1864.

Robinson, William H. *Phillis Wheatley and Her Writings*. New York: Garland, 1984.

Richmond, M.A. *Bid the Vassal Soar: Interpretive Essays on the Life and Poetry of Phillis Wheatley (ca. 1753-1784) and George Moses Horton (ca. 1797-1883)*. Washington, D.C.: Howard University Press, 1974.

Tyson, John R. *In the Midst of Early Methodism: Lady Huntingdon and Her Correspondence*.
Lanham, Md.: Scarecrow Press, 2006.

Wheatley, Phillis. *The Collected Works of Phillis Wheatley.*
New York: Oxford University Press, 1988.

Wheatley, Phillis, and Margaretta Matilda Odell, ed. *Memoir and Poems of Phillis Wheatley, a Native African and a Slave. Dedicated to the Friends of the Africans*. Boston: Geo. W. Light, 1834. Electronic Edition, University of North Carolina at Chapel Hill, 1999. http://docsouth.unc.edu/neh/wheatley/wheatley.html

Index cont.

CRITICAL THINKING USING THE COMMON CORE

1. People doubted Phillis Wheatley's writing abilities because she was an
   African-American and a woman. How do you think her writing would have
   been received if she lived today? (Integration of Knowledge and Ideas)

2. Phillis won her freedom from slavery, but her life as a free woman was
   much more difficult. Why do you think that was the case? (Integration of
   Knowledge and Ideas)

3. Phillis supported the American independence movement and wrote poetry
   about it, but the freedom and independence the war brought to American
   citizens didn't apply to her and other African-Americans. What would it
   have been like to be in that situation? Support your answer with evidence
   from the text. (Key Ideas and Details)